Finding Your Ancestors

By Beth Jane Reben and Rochelle Reben

Table of Contents

Introduction

Tracing your family tree is an exhilarating experience. Whether discovering ancestors of long ago, or finding known or unknown living relatives, there is always a new path to be explored. The possibilities are endless!

You will set off on this journey not knowing what you might find. There will be some frustrations, some dead ends, and false starts, but with perseverance and using the tools we give you in this book, you will succeed.

We will provide you with the steps you should take to embark upon your research into your family's history. While we touch briefly on foreign resources, our main focus is on research within the United States.

Our interest in genealogy began with our mother who decided to research her family. She began this arduous task before resources were readily available on the Internet. She spent countless hours and much expense visiting the genealogy library, going through documents on microfilm, and obtaining documents by mail. This was not only time consuming but also frustrating since she often ended up with documents that were not relevant to her research.

We have continued her research and have branched out to our father's family. Today, there are hundreds of websites devoted to genealogy. While the process can still be trying at times, it is easier, faster, and more efficient. The results have been thrilling.

Getting Organized

Before getting started you will want to have some materials on hand for organizing your information.

First, you will need genealogy software. You can download *Personal Ancestral File* for free at www.familysearch.org/eng/paf/pafonline.asp or purchase commercial software such as *Family Tree Maker* or *Roots Magic.* The software allows you to enter family data and create charts and reports. When using software it is essential that you back up your data on a flash drive in case of unexpected computer crashes or glitches.

Next, you will want to create a system for organizing your paper documents. We like to use binders with dividers organized by family. You could also use file folders.

Other useful items are highlighters, a magnifying glass, a recording device for family interviews, and a notebook or pad for recording notes. We also suggest that you keep a log to keep track of your research in order to avoid duplicate effort. (See example on page 2)

Research Log

Ancestor's name

Objective(s)			Locality	

Date of search	Location/ call number	Description of source (author, title, year, pages)	Comments (purpose of search, results, years and names searched)	Doc. number

Chapter 1

Start With What You Know

You know more about your family than you think. Open your genealogy software and start with yourself. Then enter the names of immediate family; parents, siblings, grandparents, aunts, uncles, cousins, etc. Include your relatives' spouses as well. The standard genealogy format is to use maiden names for women. Add as many details about each individual as possible. Include:

- date and place of birth
- date and place of baptism
- date and place of marriage
- military service
- date , place, and cause of death
- date and place of burial
- occupation
- places of residence
- date and place of immigration
- date and place of naturalization

Don't worry if you are missing information, this is what your research will focus on. Next, talk to relatives to see if they can provide more information. Go back as many generations as you can.

A great way to get your relatives involved is by using the website www.geni.com. This is a free website where you enter your family tree and can invite your relatives to join your tree. Once they join, they can add to the tree. Another great feature of geni.com is that you can find other family trees that contain your relatives. You can then combine your trees and collaborate. This website also allows you to upload documents and photos and send messages to family members.

Now it is time to search your closets, attic, garage or any other place you keep family memorabilia. You are looking for birth certificates, death certificates, naturalization papers, marriage certificates, baptismal records, photos, letters, family bibles, or anything else that will shed light on your family history. Older relatives may be able to identify unknown family members in photos.

Once you have entered as much information as you can, it is time to prepare family group sheets and descendant charts. These will give you a visual summary of what you know. You will be able to produce this with your software. We have provided a copy from our own research to give you an idea of the information they provide.

Descendant Chart for
Jack Deutsch

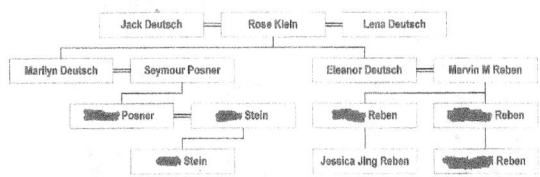

Family Group Sheet

Husband:	**Nathan Louis Rabinowitz Reben**	
Name:	Nathan Louis Rabinowitz Reben	
Gender:	Male	
Birth:	09 Oct 1892 in Minsk, Russia	
Death:	22 Jul 1979 in Queens, New York, United States	
Burial:	24 Jul 1979 in Flushing, Queens, New York, United States	
Marriage:	27 Dec 1914 in brooklyn, new york, United States	
Father:	Morris Rabinowitz	
Mother:	Minnie Kroll	
Other Spouses:	Anna Lottman (b: 06 Jul 1889)	

Wife:	**Anna Lottman**	
Name:	Anna Lottman	
Gender:	Female	
Birth:	06 Jul 1889 in New York, New York, United States	
Death:	20 May 1988 in New York, New York, United States	
Burial:		
Father:	Herman Lottman	
Mother:	Minnie Roth	
Other Spouses:		

Children:		
1	Name:	Irving Rabinowitz Reben
M	Gender:	Male
	Birth:	17 Oct 1915 in New York City, New York, United States
	Death:	Abt. Feb 1983 in Queens, New York, United States
	Burial:	
	Marriage:	
	Spouses:	Dorothy Schare (b: 16 Feb 1917)
2	Name:	Pearl Rabinowitz Reben
F	Gender:	Female
	Birth:	17 Oct 1915 in New York, New York, United States
	Death:	26 Apr 2004 in New York, Queens, New York, United States
	Burial:	
	Marriage:	
	Spouses:	Louis Altschuler (b: 14 Jan 1914)
3	Name:	Marvin M Reben
M	Gender:	Male
	Birth:	19 Sep 1924 in New York, New York, United States
	Death:	20 Mar 1999 in Banning, California, United States
	Burial:	
	Marriage:	06 Jun 1948 in New York, New York, United States
	Spouses:	Eleanor Deutsch (b: 01 Oct 1926)

Notes

Nathan Louis Rabinowitz Reben
> Person note: {geni:occupation} Newspaper Dealer

Chapter 2

Online Resources

There are more online resources available for your genealogy research than we can possibly fit into the scope of this book so we will highlight the ones we have found to be most useful. As you delve into this project you will undoubtedly come across some of your own.

Ancestry.com

We always start with ancestry.com which, as far as we know, holds the most extensive online collection of genealogy material. While there is a small fee, ancestry.com is an invaluable resource making it well worth the money. They offer a 14 day free trial so you can see what they have to offer. If you are near a Mormon family history library, they allow you to use ancestry.com. for free. You don't have to be a member of the Mormon Church to use the library. To find a family history library near you check out www.familysearch.org/locations. Ancestry.com has records from all over the world including census, birth, marriage, death, military, immigration and travel. They are constantly updating and adding records. Additionally, members upload their trees which you may search.

Family Search

Family search (www.familysearch.org) is the free genealogy website maintained by the Mormon Church. Most of it is on microfilm which can be ordered at any family history center. They are in the process of indexing all of their materials, many of which can be found online at their website. New collections are being added every day. Many of the collections contain copies of original documents. The site provides a microfilm number for those that do not have online images. While still a work in progress this promises to be an amazing free resource. We have located records here which are not accessible anywhere else online. It is worth a visit from time to time since they are constantly updating. You can also find free online genealogy courses.

Specialized Resources

Jewish Gen (www.jewishgen.org) This is the ultimate resource for Jewish genealogy. They have Jewish records from all over the world. In addition to country specific databases you can find; Family Finder, Town Finder, Holocaust Database, Burial Registry, Yizkor Books, Shtetlinks , and countless other databases too numerous to name here. Jewish Gen is essential for anyone searching for their Jewish ancestors.

Italian Genealogical Group (www.italiangen.org) While this website is primarily devoted to Italian genealogy it is also useful to those with ancestors from the New York City area. The data base includes; New York naturalizations, death records, marriage records, and birth records. There is also an Italian surname database and a Communes of Italy database. You can also find articles of interest from their newsletter.

Ellis Island (www.ellisisland.org) This website allows you to search and view passenger lists from ships which arrived at Ellis Island.

Castle Garden (www.castlegarden.org) Castle Garden was the arrival site for 11 million immigrants from 1820-1892. It was replaced by Ellis Island. There is a search engine for arrivals.

Stephen P. Morse (stevemorse.org) This site contains numerous tools for accessing genealogy records. Some of these records include; Immigration, US and Canadian Census, Calendar Conversions, Language Translation for Russian, Hebrew, Yiddish, Greek, Arabic, and Japanese, to name a few. There is a section on the Holocaust and Resources for Genetic Genealogy (DNA). Again, there are too many resources to name.

German Genealogy Group (www.germangenealogygroup.com) They have many databases relating to German genealogy. Included are church databases, naturalization, vital records from New York City, and miscellaneous New York City databases as well as German immigrant databases. The site also includes research tips.

Social Security Death Index (www.ssdi.rootsweb.ancestry.com) You can find records for deaths reported to social security since 1962. Information includes the person's social security number, date of birth and death, state of issuance of social security number, and residence at time of death. This information can be used to obtain a death certificate.

Chapter 3

Census Records

The US Constitution requires the government to conduct a census every ten years. This is very fortunate for genealogists since census records are an invaluable source for information. Census records are sealed for 72 years which means the most recent available census is from 1930. The 1940 census will be released on April 1, 2012. The 1890 census was unfortunately mostly destroyed so these records are limited. The census is a "snapshot " of the family unit for that time. A few of the questions vary from census to census but all contain names of household members, their address, ages, relationships , occupations , places of birth, citizenship, and language spoken. Some census records include date of immigration, date of naturalization, number of live children, parents' country of origin and literacy. We recommend that you search all censuses dating from your ancestors' arrival in the United States. Since family often lived near each other and the census is arranged by street address it is a good idea to check the neighbors, which is available on the same census page.

While the census can provide important information, there are some problems you should be aware of. The census was taken by a census taker who went from door to door and collected information from the people in each household. Mistakes were often made. Names were sometimes spelled incorrectly or a wrong name was written. If you are having trouble finding your ancestor, try variations on the spelling of the name. Birthdates often varied from census to census so you may need to verify these dates in some other way which we will discuss later on.

The most complete census records are on ancestry.com. Some censuses are also available on family search. When searching on ancestry.com, it is useful to search using *Soundex* which allows for variations in spellings.

Once you find your family on the census records you can start to fill in additional information in your genealogy software. The knowledge you have gained in the census will be used as a springboard toward further investigation.

Information found on each Census

We obtained this information from the website of the US Census Bureau, **www.census.gov**

1790

1. Name of head of household,
2. The number of free white males under 16 years old
3. Number of free white males 16 and over
4. Number of free white females
5. Number of other free persons
6. Number of slaves.

1800

1. Name of the county, parish, township, town, or city
2. Name of head of household
3. Number of free white males and females
4. Age, respectively: *under ten years ,of ten years but under 16, of 16 but under 26, of 26 but under 45, and 45 years and older.*
5. Number of all other free persons

6. Number of slaves

1810

Identical to 1800

1820

1. Name of the county, parish, township, town, or city
2. Name of head of household
3. Number of free white males and females
4. Age, respectively: *under 10 years ,of 10 years but under 16, of 16 but under 18 (for males)of 18 but under 26 (for males), of 16 but under 26 (for females), of 26 but under 45 ,and 45 years and older.*
5. Number of male and female slaves, age respectively: under 14, of 14 but under 26, of 26 but under 45, 45 years and above.
6. Number of free colored males and females, age respectively: *under 14, of 14 but under 26, of 26 but under 45, 45 years and above.*
7. Number of foreigner not naturalized
8. Number of persons (including slaves) engaged in agriculture ,commerce ,and manufactures

   1830

   The number of free White males and females, respectively:

   - under 5 years
   - 5 to 10 years
   - 10 to 15 years
   - 15 to 20 years
   - 20 to 30 years
   - 30 to 40 years
   - 40 to 50 years

- 50 to 60 years
- 60 to 70 years
- 70 to 80 years
- 80 to 90 years
- 90 to 100 years
- 100 years and upward
- The number of slaves and free colored persons of each sex, respectively:
  - under 10 years
  - 10 to 24 years
  - 24 to 36 years
  - 36 to 55 years
  - 55 to 100 years
  - 100 years and upward
- The number of White persons and the number of "slaves and colored persons" who were deaf and dumb aged:
  - under 14 years
  - 14 and under 25 years
  - 25 years and upward
- The number of White persons and "slaves or colored persons" who were blind, respectively
- The number of White persons who were foreigners not naturalized

1840

same as 1830

1850

The 1850 was the first time people were listed individually instead of by family. There were two separate questionnaires, one for free people and one for slaves.

Listed by column number, enumerators recorded the following information:

1. Number of dwelling house (in order visited)
2. Number of family (in order visited)
3. Name
4. Age
5. Sex
6. Color

    This column was to be left blank if a person was White, marked "B" if a person was Black, and marked "M" if a person was Mulatto.

7. Profession, occupation, or trade of each person over 15 years of age
8. Value of real estate owned by person
9. Place of Birth

    If a person was born in the United States, the enumerator was to enter the state they were born in. If the person was born outside of the United States, the enumerator was to enter their native country.

10. Was the person married within the last year?
11. Was the person at school within the last year?
12. If this person was over 20 years of age, could they not read and write?
13. Is the person "deaf, dumb, blind, insane, idiotic, pauper, or convict?"

Schedule No. 2 - Slave Inhabitants

Slaves were listed by owner, not individually. Listed by column number, enumerators recorded the following information:

1. Name of owner
2. Number of slave

    Each owner's slave was only assigned a number, not a name. Numbering restarted with each new owner

3. Age
4. Sex
5. Color

    This column was to be marked with a "B" if the slave was Black and an "M" if they were Mulatto.

18

6. Listed in the same row as the owner, the number of uncaught escaped slaves in the past year
7. Listed in the same row as the owner, the number of slaves freed from bondage in the past year
8. Is the slave "deaf and dumb, blind, insane, or idiotic?"

1860

The following were used for the free people questionnaire. The slave questionnaire was the same as the one used in 1850.

1. ;Number of dwelling home in order of visitation by the enumerator
2. Number of family in order of visitation by the enumerator
3. Name
4. Age
5. Sex
6. Color

   Enumerators could mark "W" for Whites, "B" for Blacks, or "M" for Mulattos.
7. Profession, Occupation, or Trade of each person, male and female, over 15 years of age
8. Value of person's real estate
9. Value of person's personal estate
10. Place of birth

    Enumerator could list the state, territory, or country of the person's birth
11. Was the person was married within the last year?
12. Did the person attend school within the last year?
13. If the person was over 20 years of age, could he not read or write?
14. Was the person deaf and dumb, blind, idiotic, pauper, or convict?

1870

1. Number of dwelling house, by order of visitation from enumerator
2. Number of family, by order of visitation from enumerator
3. Name
4. Age

5. Sex

6. Color

   Enumerators could mark "W" for White, "B" for Black, "M" for Mulatto, "C" for Chinese [a category which included all Asians], or "I" for American Indian.

7. Profession, occupation, or trade

8. Value of real estate

9. Value of personal estate

10. Place of birth

    State or territory of the United States or foreign country

11. Was the person's father of foreign birth?

12. Was the person's mother of foreign birth?

13. If the person was born within the last year, which month?

14. If the person was married within the last year, which month?

15. Did the person attend school within the last year?

16. Can the person not read?

17. Can the person not write?

18. Is the person deaf and dumb, blind, insane, or idiotic?

19. Is the person a male citizen of the United States of 21 years or upwards?

20. Is the person a male citizen of the United States of 21 years or upwards whose right to vote is denied or abridged on grounds other than "rebellion or other crime?"

1880

1. Number of dwelling home, in order of visitation by the enumerator

2. Number of family, in order of visitation by the enumerator

3. Name

4. Color

   Enumerators were to mark "W" for White, "B" for Black, "Mu" for Mulatto, "C" for Chinese [a category which included all east Asians], of "I" for American Indian

5. Sex

6. Age

7. If the person was born within the census year, what was the month?
8. Relationship to the head of the family
9. Is the person single?
10. Is the person married?
11. Is the person widowed or divorced?

    Enumerators were to mark "W" for widowed and "D" for divorced
12. Was the person married within the census year?
13. Profession, occupation, or trade
14. Number of months the person had been employed within the census year
15. Was, on the day of the enumerator's visit, the person was sick or disabled so as to be unable to attend to ordinary business or duties? If so, what was the sickness or disability?
16. Was the person blind?
17. Was the person deaf and dumb?
18. Was the person idiotic?
19. Was the person insane?
20. Was the person maimed, crippled, bedridden, or otherwise disabled?
21. Had the person attended school in the past year?
22. Can the person not read?
23. Can the person not write?
24. What was the person's place of birth?
25. What was the person's father's place of birth?
26. What was the person's mother's place of birth?

1890

A. Number of dwelling house in the order of visitation by enumerator
B. Number of families in the dwelling house
C. Number of persons in the dwelling house
D. Number of this family in order of visitation by enumerator
E. Number of persons in this family

The following questions, listed by row number, were asked of each individual resident:

1. Christian name in full, and initial of middle name
2. Surname
3. Was this person a soldier, sailor, or marine during the Civil War (U.S.A. or C.S.A.), or the widow of such a person?
4. Relationship to the head of the family
5. Race

   Enumerators were instructed to write "White," "Black," "Mulatto," "Quadroon," "Octoroon," "Chinese," "Japanese," or "Indian."
6. Sex
7. Age
8. Was the person single, married, widowed, or divorced?
9. Was the person married within the last year?
10. How many children was the person a mother of? How many of those children were living?
11. Person's place of birth
12. Place of birth of person's father
13. Place of birth of person's mother
14. How many years has the person been in the United States?
15. Is the person naturalized?
16. Has the person taken naturalization papers out?
17. Profession, trade, or occupation
18. Number of months unemployed in the past year
19. How many months did the person attend school in the past year?
20. Can the person read?
21. Can the person write?
22. Can the person speak English? If not, what language does he speak?
23. Is the person suffering from an acute chronic disease? If so, what is the name of that disease and the length of time affected?
24. Is the person defective of mind, sight, hearing, or speech? Is the person crippled, maimed, or deformed? If yes, what was the name of his defect?
25. Is the person a prisoner, convict, homeless child, or pauper?
26. Depending on the person's status in the questions in rows 22, 23, or 24, the enumerator would indicate on this line whether additional information was recorded about him on a special schedule

The following questions, located at the end of each family's questionnaire sheet were asked of each family and farm visited:

26. Was the home the family lived in hired, or was it owned by the head or by a member of the family?

27. If owned by a member of the family, was the home free from "mortgage encumbrance?"

28. If the head of the family was a farmer, was the farm which he cultivated hired or was it owned by him or a member of his family?

29. If owned by the head or member of the family, was the farm free from "mortgage incumbrance?"

30. If the home or farm was owned by the head or member of the family, and mortgaged, what was the post office address of the owner?

1900

For the first time additional questions were asked of the American Indians.

General Population Schedule

1. Number of dwelling home in order of visitation by enumerator
2. Number of family in order of visitation by enumerator
3. Name
4. Relation to head of the family
5. Color or Race

    Enumerators were to mark "W" for White, "B" for Black, "Ch" for Chinese, "Jp" for Japanese, or "In" for American Indian.

6. Sex
7. Date of Birth
8. Age
9. Was the person single, married, widowed, or divorced?
10. How many years has the person been married?
11. For mothers, how many children has the person had?
12. How many of those children are living?
13. What was the person's place of birth?
14. What was the person's father's place of birth?
15. What was the person's mother's place of birth?
16. What year did the person immigrate to the United States?

17. How many years has the person been in the United States?
18. Is the person naturalized?
19. Occupation, trade, or profession
20. How many months has the person not been employed in the past year?
21. How many months did the person attend school in the past year?
22. Can the person read?
23. Can the person write?
24. Can the person speak English?
25. Is the person's home owned or rented?
26. If it is owned, is the person's home owned free or mortgaged?
27. Does the person live in a farm or in a house?
28. If a person lived on a farm, the enumerator was to write that farm's identification number on its corresponding agricultural questionnaire in this column

Indian Population Schedule
29. Indian Name
30. Tribe of this person
31. Tribe of this person's father
32. Tribe of this person's mother
33. Fraction of person's lineage that is white
34. Is this person living in polygamy?
35. Is this person taxed?

An American Indian was considered "taxed" if he or she was detached from his or her tribe and was living in the White community and subject to general taxation, or had been allotted land by the federal government and thus acquired citizenship.
36. If this person has acquired American citizenship, what year?
37. Did this person acquire citizenship by receiving an allotment of land from the federal government?
38. Is this person's house "movable" or "fixed?"

Enumerators were to mark "movable" if the person lived in a tent, tepee, or other temporary structure; they were to mark "fixed" if he or she lived in a permanent dwelling of any kind.

1910

1. Relationship to head of the family
2. Sex
3. Color or Race

   Enumerators were to enter "W" for White, "B" for Black, "Mu" for mulatto, "Ch" for Chinese, "Jp" for Japanese, "In" for American Indian, or "Ot" for other races.

4. Age
5. Is the person single, married, widowed, or divorced?

   Enumerators were to enter "S" for single, "Wd" for widowed, "D" for divorced, "M1" for married persons in their first marriage, and "M2" for those married persons in their second or subsequent marriage.

6. Number of years of present marriage
7. How many children is the person the mother of?
8. Of the children a person has mothered, how many are still alive?
9. Place of birth of the person
10. Place of birth of the person's father
11. Place of birth of the person's mother
12. Year of immigration to the United States
13. Is the person naturalized or an alien?
14. Can the person speak English? If not, what language does the person speak?
15. The person's trade, profession, or occupation
16. General nature of the industry, business, or establishment in which this person works
17. Is the person an employer, employee, or working on his own account?
18. If the person is an employee, was he out of work on April 15, 1910?
19. If the person is an employee, what is the number of weeks he was out of work in 1909?
20. Can the person read?
21. Can the person write?
22. Has the person attended school at any time since September, 1909?
23. Is the person's home owned or rented?

24. Is the person's home owned free or mortgaged?
25. Does the person reside in a home or on a farm?
26. If on a farm, what is the farm's identification number on the census farm schedule?
27. Is the person a survivor of the Union or Confederate Army or Navy?
28. Is the person blind in both eyes?
29. Is the person deaf and dumb?

Indian Population Schedule

1. Tribe of this person
2. Tribe of this person's father
3. Tribe of this person's mother
4. Proportion of this person's lineage that is American Indian
5. Proportion of this person's lineage that is white
6. Proportion of this person's lineage that is black
7. Number of times married
8. Is this person living in polygamy?
9. If this person is living in polygamy, are his wives sisters?
10. If this person graduated from an educational institution, which one?
11. Is this person a taxed?

    An American Indian was considered "taxed" if he or she was detached from his or her tribe and was living in the white community and subject to general taxation, or had been allotted land by the federal government and thus acquired citizenship.
12. If this person had received an allotment of land from the government, what was the year of that allotment?
13. Is this person residing on his or her own land?
14. Is this person living in a "civilized" or "aboriginal" dwelling?

    Enumerators were to mark "Civ." (for "civilized") if the person was living in a log, frame, brick, or stone house, etc. and "Abor." (for "aboriginal") if the person was living in a tent, tepee, cliff dwelling, etc.

1920

1. Street of person's place of abode

2. House number or farm
3. Number of dwelling house in order of visitation by enumerator
4. Number of family in order of visitation by enumerator
5. Name
6. Relationship to head of family
7. Is the person's home owned or rented?
8. If owned, is it owned freely or mortgaged?
9. Sex
10. Color or race

    Enumerators were to enter "W" for White, "B" for Black, "Mu" for mulatto, "Ch" for Chinese, "Jp" for Japanese, "In" for American Indian, or "Ot" for other races.

11. Age at last birthday
12. Single, married, widowed, or divorced?

    Enumerators were to enter "S" for single, "Wd" for widowed, "D" for divorced, "M1" for married persons in their first marriage, and "M2" for those married persons in their second or subsequent marriage.

13. Year of immigration to the United States
14. Is the person naturalized or alien?
15. If naturalized, what was the year of naturalization?
16. Did the person attend school at any time since September 1, 1919?
17. Can the person read?
18. Can the person write?
19. Person's place of birth
20. Person's mother tongue
21. Person's father's place of birth
22. Person's father's mother tongue
23. Person's mother's place of birth
24. Person's mother's mother tongue
25. Can the person speak English?
26. Person's trade or profession

27. Industry, business, or establishment in which the person works
28. Is the person an employer, a salary or wage worker, or working on his own account?
29. If the person is a farmer, what is the farm's identification number on the corresponding farm schedule?

1930

Population Schedule
1. Street the enumerated person lives on
2. House number of enumerated person (in cities and towns)
3. Number of dwelling house in order of visitation by enumerator
4. Number of family in order of visitation by enumerator
5. Name
6. Relationship to head of family
7. Is the person's home owned or rented?
8. If the home is owned, is it owned free or mortgaged?
9. Does this person live on a farm NOW?
10. Did this person live on a farm A YEAR AGO?
11. Sex
12. Color or Race
    Enumerators were to enter "W" for white, "Neg" for black, "Mex" for Mexican, "In" for American Indian, "Ch" for Chinese, "Jp" for Japanese, "Fil" for Filipino, "Hin" for Hindu, and "Kor" for Korean. All other races were to be written out in full.
13. Age
14. Is the person single, married, divorced, or widowed?
15. Has the person attended school at any time since Sept. 1, 1929?
16. Can the person read and write?
17. Person's place of birth
18. Person's father's place of birth
19. Person's mother's place of birth
20. Year of immigration into the United States
21. Is the person naturalized or an alien?
22. Is the person able to speak English?
23. Trade, profession, or particular kind of work done?
24. Industry or business in which at work

25. Is person an Employee (E), wage or salary worker (W), or own account (O)?

26. Whether the person is actually at work?

27. Record line number for unemployed

28. Whether the person is a veteran of the U.S. military or naval forces mobilized for any war or expedition?

29. If yes, which war or expedition?
Enumerators were to enter "WW" for World War I, "Sp" for the Spanish-American War, "Civ" for the Civil War, "Phil" for the Phillipine insurrection, "Box" for the Boxer rebellion, or "Mex" for the Mexican expedition.

30. Number of farm schedule

Census of Unemployment

Enumerators were instructed to fill out an additional questionnaire for all gainful workers who were not at work the on the workday before enumeration. This special schedule collected the following information, organized by column number:

1. Date of enumeration

2. Sheet number of person's corresponding population schedule entry

3. Line number of person's corresponding population schedule entry

4. Name

5. Does this person usually work at a gainful occupation?

6. Does this person usually have a job of any kind?

If this person has a job...

7. How many weeks since he has worked at that job?

8. Why was he not at work yesterday (or the last regular workday)? Enumerators were instructed to be as specific as possible. A list of examples provided to enumerators included: "sickness," "was laid off," "voluntary lay-off," "bad weather," "lack of materials," "strike," etc.

9. Does he lose a day's pay by not being at work?

10. How many days did he work last week?

11. How many days does he work in a full-time week?

If this person has no job of any kind...

12. Is he able to work?

13. Is he looking for a job?

14. For how many weeks has he been without a job?
15. Reason for being out of a job
    Enumerators were instructed to be as specific as possible. A list of examples provided to enumerators included: "plant closed down," "sickness," "off season," "job completed," "machines introduced," "strike," etc.

Supplemental Schedule for Indian Population

The additional questions asked of American Indians were much less numerous than in past censuses. The following information, listed by column number, was collected:

1. Sheet number of person's corresponding population schedule entry
2. Line number of person's corresponding population schedule entry
3. Name
4. Sex
5. Age
6. Is the person of full American Indian or mixed lineage?
7. Tribe
8. Person's Post Office address
9. Agency where the person is enrolled

For future reference, here are the questions asked in the 1940 census.

1940 (Population)

"The 1940 census was the first to include a statistical sample. Five percent of people were asked an additional 16 questions. In order to gauge the effect of the Great Depression on the nation's housing stock, a census of occupied dwellings was coupled with the usual demographic questions. Enumerators collected the following information, organized by column number:"

Population
1. Street the person lives on
2. House number
3. Number of household in order of visitation
4. Is the home owned or rented?
5. Value of the home, if owned, or monthly rental, if rented

6. Does the person's household live on a farm?
7. Name
8. Relationship with the head of household
9. Sex
10. Color or race
11. Age at last birthday
12. Marital status
13. Did the person attend school or college at any time in the past year?
14. What was the highest grade of school that the person completed?
15. Person's place of birth
16. If foreign born, is the person a citizen?

17. City, town, or village
    o   For villages with fewer than 2,600 residents, and all unorganized places, enumerators were to enter "R."
18. County
19. State or Territory
20. Was this house on a farm?

For persons 14 years and older - employment status

21. Was the person at work for pay or profit in private or nonemergency government work during the week of March 24 - 30?
22. If not, was he at work on, or assigned to, public emergency work (WPA, NYA, CCC, etc.) during the week of March 24 - 30?
23. If the person was neither at work or assigned public emergency work: was this person seeking work?
24. If not seeking work, did he have a job or business?
25. For persons answering "No" to questions 21, 22, 23, and 24; indicate whether engaged in home housework (H), in school (S), unable to work (U), or Other (Ot)
26. If the person was at work in private or non emergency government employment: how many hours did he work in the week of March 24 - 30?
27. If the person was seeking work or assigned to public emergency work: what was the duration, in weeks, of his unemployment?
28. What is the person's occupation, trade, or profession?

29. What is the person's industry or business?

30. What is the person's class of worker?

31. Number of weeks worked in 1939 (or equivalent of full time weeks)

32. Amount of money, wages, or salary received (including commissions)

33. Did this person receive income of more than $50 from sources other than money wages or salary?

34. Corresponding number on the Farm Schedule of the person's farm

Supplementary Questions
35. Name

36. Person's father's birthplace

37. Person's mother's birthplace

38. Person's mother or native tongue

Veterans

Is this person a veteran of the United States military forces; or the wife, widow, or under-18-year old child of a veteran?

39. If so enter "Yes"

40. If the person is a child of a veteran, is the veteran father dead?

41. War or military service
Enumerators were to mark "W" for World War I; "S" for the Spanish-American War, the Phillipine insurrection, or Boxer Rebellion; "SW" for both the Spanish-American War and World War I; "R" for peacetime service only; or "Ot" for any other war or expedition

For persons 14 years old and over

Social Security
42. Does this person have a federal Social Security number?

43. Were deductions for federal Old-Age Insurance or railroad retirement made from this person's wages in 1939?

44. If so, were deductions made from all, one-half or more, or less than one-half of the person's wages or salary?

45. What is this person's usual occupation?

46. What is this person's usual industry?

47. What class of worker is this person?

For all women who are or have been married

48. Has this person been married more than once?

32

49. Age at first marriage
50. Number of children ever born

1940 (Housing)
Census of Occupied Dwellings

Location and Household Data

1. Number of structure in order of visitation by enumerator
   Dwelling Unit number within structure
2. Line number on the corresponding population questionnaire
   Block Number
   Name of head of family
   Street number and address
   Apartment number or location
3. Color or race of head
   - o 1.) White
   - o 2.) Black
   - o 3.) All other races
4. Number of persons in household
5. Does this family live on a farm?
   - o 1.) Yes
   - o 0.) No
6. What is this family's home tenure?
   - o 0.) Owned
   - o 1.) Rented
7. Value of home of monthly rental (in dollars)
   Estimated rent of owned non-farm home (in dollars)

II. Characteristics of Structure

8. Type of structure in which this dwelling unit is located
   - o Structure without business
     - ▪ V.) 1-family detached
     - ▪ 0.) 1-family attached
     - ▪ 1.) 2-family side-by-side
     - ▪ 2.) 2-family other

- o 3-or-more-family structure without business (list number of units)
- o Structure with business
- o Other dwelling place

9. Originally built as:
   - o 1.) Residential structure with the same current number of dwelling units
   - o 2.) Residential structure with a different from the current number of dwelling units
   - o 3.) Non-residential structure

10. Exterior material
    - o 1.) Wood
    - o 2.) Brick
    - o 3.) Stucco
    - o 4.) Other

11. Is the structure in need of major repair?
    - o 1.) Yes
    - o 0.) No

12. Year originally built

13. Number of rooms

14. Water Supply
    - o 1.) Running water in dwelling unit
    - o 2.) Hand pump in dwelling unit
    - o 3.) Running water within 50 feet of dwelling unit
    - o 4.) Other supply within 50 feet of dwelling unit
    - o 5.) No water supply within 50 feet of dwelling unit

15. Toilet facilities
    - o 1.) Flush toilet in structure, in exclusive use
    - o 2.) Flush toilet in structure, shared
    - o 3.) Non-flush toilet in structure
    - o 4.) Outside toilet or privy
    - o 5.) No toilet or privy

16. Bathtub or shower with running water in structure
    - o 1.) Exclusive use
    - o 2.) Shared
    - o 3.) None

17. Principle lighting equipment
    - 1.) Electric
    - 2.) Gas
    - 3.) Kerosene/Gasoline
    - 4.) Other
18. Principle refrigeration equipment
    - 1.) Mechanical
    - 2.) Ice
    - 3.) Other
    - 4.) None
19. Radio in dwelling unit?
    - 1.) Yes
    - 0.) No
20. Heating equipment
    - 1.) Steam or hot water system
    - 2.) Piped warm air system
    - 3.) Pipeless warm air furnace
    - 4.) Heating stove
    - 5.) Other or none
21. Principal fuel used for heating
    - 1.) Coal or coke
    - 2.) Wood
    - 3.) Gas
    - 4.) Electric
    - 5.) Fuel Oil
    - 6.) Kerosene/Gasoline
    - 7.) Other
    - 8.) None
22. Principal fuel used for cooking
    - 1.) Coal or coke
    - 2.) Wood
    - 3.) Gas
    - 4.) Electric
    - 6.) Kerosene/Gasoline
    - 7.) Other

- o 8.) None
23. Is furniture included in the cost of rent?
    - o 1.) Yes
    - o 0.) No
    - o Estimated cost of rent without furniture (in dollars)
24. Average monthly cost of...
    - o Electricity
    - o Gas
    - o Other fuel
    - o Water
25. Value of property (in dollars)
    Number of dwelling units on property
26. Is there a mortgage on the property?
    - o 1.) Yes
    - o 0.) No
    - o Present debt
        - ▪ On 1st mortgage (in dollars)
        - ▪ On 2nd mortgage (in dollars)
27. Are Regular payments required...
    - o 1.) Monthly?
    - o 2.) Quarterly?
    - o 3.) Semi-annually?
    - o 4.) Annually?
    - o 5.) On another regular payment plan?
    - o 6.) On no regular payment plan
    - o Amount of each payment (in dollars)
28. Do payments include an amount for the reduction of principal?
    - o 1.) Yes
    - o 0.) No
29. Do payments include real estate taxes?
    - o 1.) Yes
    - o 0.) No
30. Interest rate now being charged (in percentages)
31. Holder of the first mortgage (or land contract)
    - o 1.) Building and loan

- o 2.) Commercial bank
- o 3.) Savings bank
- o 4.) Life insurance company
- o 5.) Mortgage company
- o 6.) Home Owner's Loan Corporation
- o 7.) Individual
- o 8.) Other

Chapter 4

Vital Records

Vital records are a primary source for validating what you may already know and adding additional details about your family member. These records include original birth, marriage , and death certificates. Although you might already know the dates of these important events, it is well worth it to obtain these original documents since they contain more family information.

Birth Certificates:

Birth certificates typically contain not only the full name of your ancestor but also the names of the parents including mother's maiden name. You will also find the address where the family was living at the time of the birth. In addition, it will give you the exact place of birth and the name of the doctor who delivered the baby.

You will need to know the approximate date of birth as well as the location since the birth records are kept locally. There are several ways of obtaining the date of birth. You may already have that knowledge within your family or you can obtain it from the census, military records, social security death index , marriage certificates or death certificates. For New York City births, Italian gen , discussed above , has a partial searchable index which will give you the birth certificate number. Family search also has some birth records.

Many birth records are available on microfilm at the Family History Library. They can also be ordered directly for a fee from the locality where the birth took place. Some localities will do a search for you if you have a range of dates. Forms for ordering birth certificates are available online. Just Google the locality where the birth occurred. Depending on the location, these records are held at either the municipal, county, or state level.

Marriage Certificates

Marriage certificates contain the full names of the bride and groom and their dates and locations of birth. They also will give you the addresses of where they were living at the time of the marriage and their occupations.   Pay attention to the names of the witnesses as they are often family members. The bride's and groom's parents are listed as well.

Death Records

We have found that death certificates provide a lot of useful information. You will be able to find the exact date of death, the address of your relative at the time of death, and the name of your relative's parents including mother's maiden name. The information is provided by an informant who is usually a relative. The name and address of the informant will usually be stated on the certificate. Be careful about the information since it is based on the knowledge of the informant which may or may not be accurate. Some death certificates may also include your relative's occupation, place and date of birth, the cause of death, and the place of burial.

The place of burial can lead you to other family members who may be buried in the same place. Some cemeteries have an online search feature which enables you to find out whether any other relatives are buried there. If you are able to, we recommend that you visit the cemetery since gravestones may also contain useful information. A helpful online site for finding ancestor graves is www.findagrave.com. There are actual pictures of gravestones on this site. If your ancestor was Jewish, try the Jewishgen Online Worldwide Burial Registry which is a data base of more than 1.7 million names from Jewish cemeteries.

You will need to establish an approximate date of death and the place of death in order to obtain a death certificate. One way to do this is to use the Social Security Death Index. You can either access the Social Security Death Index through ancestry.com or go directly to ssdi.rootsweb.ancestry.com. Use the advanced search feature to put in the information that you know in order to narrow your search. This site can only be used for relatives who died after 1962. If you are looking for relatives who died before 1962, you have other resources available to you.

One way is to check ancestry.com. If your relative died in New York City, check the death records search on Italiangen. You might also be able to locate them in obituaries in local newspaper archives . Some of these can be found online.

Death records are maintained by the locality in which the death occurred. Do an online search to find information for your locality. Each place has their own set of directions on how to obtain death certificates.

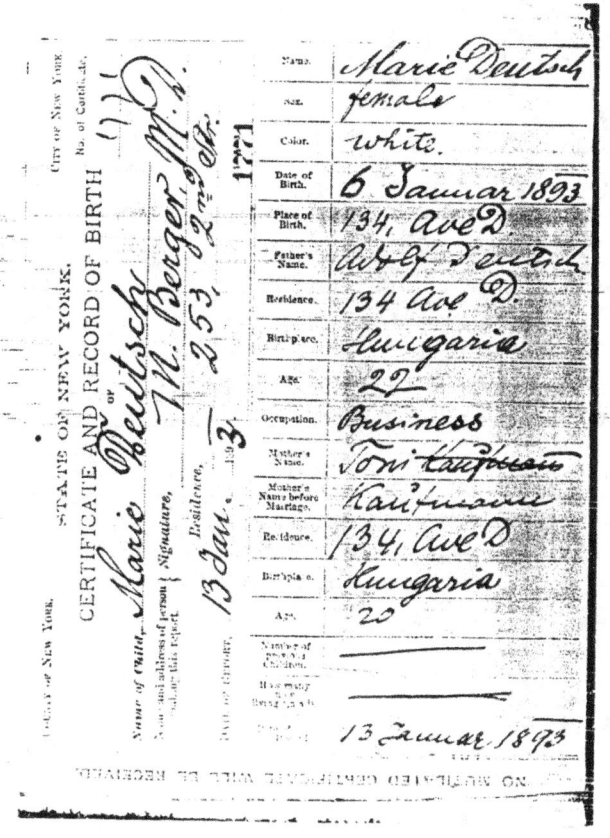

STATE OF NEW YORK.

County of New York.   City of New York.

No. of Certificate. 1771

CERTIFICATE AND RECORD OF BIRTH

Name of Child, *Marie Deutsch*

Name and address of person   Signature, *M. Berger M.D.*
making this Report.   Residence, *253, 2nd St.*

Date of Report, *13 Jan. 93*

Name.	Marie Deutsch
Sex.	female
Color.	white.
Date of Birth.	6 Januar 1893
Place of Birth.	134, Ave D
Father's Name.	Adolf Deutsch
Residence.	134 Ave D
Birthplace.	Hungaria
Age.	22
Occupation.	Business
Mother's Name.	Toni Kaufman
Mother's Name before Marriage.	Kaufmann
Residence.	134, Ave D
Birthplace.	Hungaria
Age.	20
Number of Children.	
How many now living.	
Date.	13 Januar 1893

NO MUTILATED CERTIFICATE WILL BE RECEIVED.

41

CERTIFICATE OF DEATH

Certificate No. 156-88- 4 0 6 6 8 2

1. NAME OF DECEASED *Anna*   *Reben*

(Type or Print)   (First Name)   (Middle Name)   (Last Name)

MEDICAL CERTIFICATE OF DEATH *(To be filled in by the Physician)*

2. PLACE OF DEATH	NEW YORK CITY	2b. Name of hospital or other facility if not facility, street address		2c. If in Hospital or Other Facility (Check)	2d. If inpatient, date of current admission
	2a. BOROUGH *Queens*	*The Parkway Hospital*		1 ☐ DOA 3 ☐ Outpatient 2 ☐ Emerg. 4 ☒ Inpatient	Month 5 / Day 12 / Year 88

3a. Date and Hour (Month) *May* (Day) *22* (Year) *1988*   3b. HOUR *12:45* ☒ AM ☐ PM   4. SEX *female*   5. APPROXIMATE AGE *95*

6. I HEREBY CERTIFY THAT: (Check One)

☒ I attended the deceased   ☐ A staff physician of this institution attended the deceased

☐ Dr. _____ attended the deceased

from *07-10-1976* to *5-22-1988* and last saw her alive at *8 A* M

on *05-21-1988*. I further certify that traumatic injury or poisoning DID NOT play any part in causing death, and that death did not occur in any unusual manner and was due entirely to NATURAL CAUSES.

*See first instruction on reverse of certificate.

Witness my hand this *22* day of *May* 1988 Signature *Reben* D.O. M.D.

Name of Physician *H S. PATEL* (Type or Print) Address *144.04 45th Ave, Flushing N.Y. 1355*

PERSONAL PARTICULARS *(To be filled in by Funeral Director)*

7. Usual Residence State *New York*	7b. County *Queens*	7c. City, Town, or Location *Forest Hills*	7d. Street & House No. *71-30*	Zip *110 ST.*	Apt. No.	7e. Inside City Limits of 7c ☒ Yes ☐ No

8. Served in U.S. Armed Forces: No ☒ Yes ☐ Specify years From ___ To ___

9. Marital Status (Check One) 1 ☐ Never Married 2 ☒ Widowed 3 ☐ Married or separated 4 ☐ Divorced

10. Name of Surviving Spouse (If wife, give maiden name)

11. Date of birth (Month) *July* (Day) *4* (Year) *1890*	12. Age at last birthday *97*	If under 1 Year / If less than 1 Day mos. days hours min.	13. Social Security No. *110-10-4006-D*

14a. Usual Occupation (Kind of work done during most of working lifetime, do not enter retired) *Housewife*   14b. Kind of Business

15. Birthplace (City & State or Foreign Country) *New York*   16. Education (Check only one) 0-11 ☐ 12 ☒ 13-15 ☐ 16 ☐ 17+ ☐ 0 ☐ 1 ☐ 2 ☐ 3 ☐ 4 ☐ 5 ☐

17. Other name(s) by which decedent was known

18. NAME OF FATHER OF DECEDENT *Herman Lottman*   19. MAIDEN NAME OF MOTHER OF DECEDENT

20a. NAME OF INFORMANT *Marvin Reben*	20b. RELATIONSHIP TO DECEASED *Son*	20c. ADDRESS *17 Hamilton St.*	(City) *Rockville Center*	(State) *N.Y.*	(Zip) *11570*

21a. NAME OF CEMETERY OR CREMATORY *Mt. Hebron*   21b. LOCATION (City, Town, State and Country) *Flushing, N.Y.*   21c. DATE OF BURIAL OR CREMATION *5/23/88*

22a. FUNERAL DIRECTOR *Guttermans Inc.*   22b. ADDRESS *175 N. Long Beach Rd. Rockville Center, N.Y.*

BUREAU OF VITAL RECORDS   DEPARTMENT OF HEALTH   THE CITY OF NEW YORK

VR16 (1/88)

DATE ISSUED **MAY 25 1988**   DOCUMENT NO. B 450794

VR134-275M-8-119082

STATE OF NEW YORK

CERTIFICATE AND RECORD OF MARRIAGE

No. of Certificate 438

Nathan L. Rabinowitz and Anna Lottman

	Groom		Bride
Residence	312 East 119 St. N.Y.	Residence	968 Gates ave
Age	22	Age	22
Color	White	Color	White
Single, Widowed or Divorced	Single	Single, Widowed or Divorced	Single
Occupation	News Dealer		
Birthplace	Russia	Birthplace	New Bern N.Y.
Father's Name	Morris	Father's Name	Herman
Mother's Maiden Name	Minnie Kraft	Mother's Maiden Name	Minnie Reeder
Number of Groom's Marriage	First	Number of Bride's Marriage	First

I hereby certify that the above-named groom and bride were joined in Marriage by me, in accordance with
the Laws of the State of New York, at 968 Gates ave
Borough of Brooklyn , City of New York, this 27 of December 1917

Signature of person performing the Ceremony: Rev. Morris Schechter
Official Station: 534 Williams ave
Residence: 340 Lafayette ave

Witnesses to the Marriage: {
Max Miller
Isador Ehkin
}

43

Chapter 5

Military Records

Ancestry.com has military records going back to the Revolutionary War and includes The War of 1812, The Civil War, World War I, World War II, Korea, and Vietnam. There is also a database of veteran's gravesites.

Listed below are the major collections for each war.

Revolutionary War

1. US Revolutionary War Rolls 1775-1783

2. Abstracts of Graves of Revolutionary War Patriots

3. US Compiled Revolutionary War Military Service Records, 1775-1783

4. Revolutionary War Pension and Bounty-Land Warrant Application Files, 1800-1900

5. Massachusetts Soldiers and Sailors in the Revolutionary War

6. Daughters of the American Revolution Lineage Books

7. Revolutionary War Offices

War of 1812

War of 1812 Service Records

Civil War

1. US Civil War Soldiers, 1861-1865

2. US Civil War Soldiers Records and Profiles

3. American Civil War Soldiers

4. Civil War Pension Index : General Index to Pension Files

5. US Civil War POW Records

6. US Colored Troops Military Service Records, 1861-1865

7. Alabama Civil War Muster Rolls

8. Confederate Service Records , 1861-1865

9. Confederate Applications for Presidential Pardons, 1865-1867

10. US Civil War Photos

World War I

1. World War I Draft Registration Cards, 1917-1918: includes full name, home address, date and place of birth, age, race, country of citizenship, occupation and employer, physical description, and name and address of nearest relative.

2. US WWI Mother's Pilgrimage: includes the names of widows and mothers entitled to make the US government sponsored pilgrimage to visit their loved ones' grave in Europe.

3. WWI , WWII, and Korean War Casualty Listings

World War II

1. Prisoners of the Japanese, 1941-1945

2. World War II Draft Registration Cards (During WWII, the government required registration of all men born between 1877 and 1897)

3. World War II Missing in Action or Lost at Sea

4. US World War II Army Enlistment Records

Korea

1. Casualties

Vietnam

1. Vietnam War: US Military Casualties

2. Vietnam War Awards and Decorations of Honor

The National Archives, (**aad.archives.gov/aad/index.jsp**) is another source for military records through the Vietnam War. It also includes Cold War and Diplomatic Records.

The United State Department of Veteran Affairs (**gravelocator.cem.va.gov**) contains a searchable database of all military cemeteries. It includes not only the veterans but also the names of spouses who are buried there.

Chapter 6

Immigration

Unless you are a full blooded Native American, your ancestors were immigrants. Ancestory.com has an extensive collection of passenger lists going back to the 1500s. While the earlier records are not as complete as later ones, you might get lucky and find your ancestor. Records beginning with Castle Gardens arrivals are more complete. With a bit of patience you will probably be able to find your ancestor. When searching for relatives on passenger lists, keep in mind that many immigrants switched to more American sounding names upon arrival but the passenger list name is their original name. This often poses a challenge in finding your family member.

While earlier records simply name the passenger name, age and place of origin, the Ellis Island records provide more extensive information. In addition to the name, age, and place of origin, you may be able to discover occupation in the old country, who paid for the passage as well as the name and address of the relative in the United States whom they intended to join. The name of the relatives in the US is a particularly useful piece of information. Not only does it help you differentiate between immigrants with the same name but it also provides the address where the relative was living. After all, their relative is your relative!

We were able to find our family on a document called *Record of Detained Alien Passengers.* Using this document, we learned further details, including how many meals our family ate while at Ellis Island and what time they were released.

Many European immigrants, particularly those from Eastern Europe, traveled first to Hamburg, Germany. They may have traveled by train or wagon from their village. The Hamburg port is the only port we have come across which kept track of departures. If your family came from Eastern Europe you should look for them on the Hamburg List. Sometimes immigrants took more than one ship. We found some of our family members on a ship from Hamburg to Liverpool and then another ship from Liverpool to New York, while other family members came directly from Hamburg to New York.

Chapter 7

Naturalization

Prior to 1906, naturalization could take place in any court. There were a variety of forms used that contained various pieces of information. After 1906, there were three forms in use.

The first form is called *Declaration of Intention.* This form included personal information about the immigrant including the date and place of immigration as well as the name of the ship he or she arrived on.

The *Petition for Citizenship* was the formal application for naturalization. It included basic information about the immigrant including date and place of birth and date of arrival. The petition also required a declaration by a witness. Often times that witness was a family member.

The *Certificate of Naturalization* is the final document which included the name of the individual, the name of the court , and the date of issue.

Some original documents are available on ancestry.com but generally they need to be ordered from the National Archives, *www.archives.gov.*

Ancestry.com has an extensive collection of *naturalization indexes.* These indexes contain a lot of valuable information including the name of the court, date of naturalization, address, occupation, date of birth, former nationality, port of arrival, date of arrival, and the name, address , and occupation of the witness.

R 153

Family Name	Given Name or Names
RABINOWITZ	JOSHUA

Title and Location of Court

U. S. DISTRICT COURT, NEW YORK, N.Y.

Date of Naturalization	Volume or Bundle No.	Page No.	Copy of Record No.
NOV. 23 - 1901	111	—	208

Address of Naturalized Person

242 E. 89 ST. MAN. N.Y. CITY

Occupation	Birth Date or Age	Former Nationality
SHOEMAKER	APR. 22 - 1879	RUSSIAN

Port of Arrival in the United States	Date of Arrival
N.Y. N.Y.	JULY 10 - 1896

Names, Addresses and Occupations of Witnesses To Naturalization

1. MAX JANOWITZ 242 E. 89TH ST.
2. STORE KEEPER MAN. N.Y.C.

Chapter 8

Finding Living Relatives

The thrill of finding living relatives is beyond description. There are several reasons why this is useful. They are a great source of information and can help fill in gaps in your tree. Older relatives can share interesting stories about family members and can identify unknown people in old photographs. When we connected with our mother's cousin, it was interesting to hear familiar stories we had grown up with as well as learn new ones.

Both ancestry.com and geni.com contain features which help you find people whose trees contain some of your relatives. We have located several family members in this way.

Another method is to do a Google search for people you believe may still be alive. Online White Pages have also proven to be useful.

You may also find your relatives on Facebook. We have become Facebook friends with many of our relatives. Although we have never met, we are getting to know each other.

Chapter 9

Concluding Thoughts

Once you become involved in genealogy you will find it addicting. Each new bit of information you obtain brings about new avenues to explore and new questions to answer. We hope we have provided you with the tools you need to get started on this exciting journey. Good luck in your quest!

www.ingramcontent.com/pod-product-compliance
Lightning Source LLC
Chambersburg PA
CBHW070223290526

45789CB00004B/1513